W9-AYW-053

THE ORANGUTAN

BY
CARL R. GREEN
WILLIAM R. SANFORD

EDITED BY
DR. HOWARD SCHROEDER, Ph.D.
Professor in Reading and Language Arts
Dept. of Curriculum and Instruction
Mankato State University

CRESTWOOD HOUSE
Mankato, Minnesota

LIBRARY OF CONGRESS CATALOGING IN PUBLICATION DATA
Green, Carl R.
The orangutan.

(Wildlife, habits & habitat)
SUMMARY: Describes the physical characteristics, habits, and natural environment of the orangutan.
1. Orangutan--Juvenile literature. (1. Orangutan. 2. Apes.) I. Sanford, William R. (William Reynolds). II. Title. III. Series.
QL737.P96G75   1987   599.88'42   87-19811
ISBN 0-89686-335-2

International Standard Book Number:	Library of Congress Catalog Card Number:
Library Binding 0-89686-335-2	87-19811

CREDITS

Illustrations:
Cover Photo: Nancy Adams/Tom Stack & Associates
N.H. Cheatham/DRK Photo: 5
Nadine Orabona/Stock Concepts: 6, 41
Lynn M. Stone: 9, 10, 29, 32
Rod Allin/Tom Stack & Associates: 13
Adrienne T. Gibson/Tom Stack & Associates: 14, 18, 23, 31, 36, 43
Mickey Gibson/Tom Stack & Associates: 21
Bob McKeever/Tom Stack & Associates: 24-25
Phil and Loretta Hermann: 38
Alan G. Nelson/Hillstrom Stock Photos: 44
Andy Schlabach: 45
Graphic Design & Production:
Baker Street Productions, Ltd.

CRESTWOOD HOUSE
Hwy. 66 South, Box 3427
Mankato, MN 56002-3427

TABLE OF CONTENTS

INTRODUCTION:

Dear Mark:

Do you remember my last letter? That was the one I wrote just after my dad took me to the Space Museum. Forget what I said about becoming an astronaut. My class took a field trip to the zoo today, and now I really know what I want to do. I'm going to be a naturalist! After I graduate from college, I'll go to Borneo to study orangutans.

Ms. Chang was our guide at the zoo. She told us about all the animals, but she liked the orangutans best. We spent a long time watching them. The males made me laugh—they were so fat! Ms. Chang says that's because they eat too much and don't get enough exercise.

I thought all apes were black, but orangutans are a pretty reddish-brown. Did you know that orangs (that's short for orangutans) live only in Indonesia, on the islands of Sumatra and Borneo? If you didn't, that's not surprising. No one knew very much about them before the 1960's.

Ms. Chang told us about an English naturalist who made the first good study of orangs. John MacKinnon was certain he could succeed where other naturalists

Orangutans are fun to watch.

had failed. He didn't wait for the shy "red apes" to come to him. Instead, MacKinnon followed his orangutans for weeks. Wherever they went, he was there, taking notes on their behavior.

MacKinnon was very brave. When the big males first saw him, they tried to frighten him away. They roared and glared, and charged straight at him. Some females threw sticks and branches. When MacKinnon didn't run away, the orangutans gave up and left him alone. I hope I'll have enough courage to face up to an angry orangutan some day. Ms. Chang says they're very strong.

Some people call orangutans "red apes."

The rain forest is full of dangerous wild animals. One night was especially scary for MacKinnon. He went to sleep, but woke up when he heard a series of loud crashes. An elephant was heading straight for him! MacKinnon tried another spot, only to come face-to-face with an angry porcupine.

In time, MacKinnon set up a camp where he could rest after his long trips into the forest. With the help of some natives, he built a house on stilts at the edge of a river. He kept his supplies and his collection of plants there. Every few days, he hiked deep into the forest to continue his work.

MacKinnon's fiancee joined him a few years later. After they were married, they went into the forest to study orangutans.

The MacKinnons soon had a son. They named him Jamie. One day, MacKinnon took the young boy into the forest. The orangutans were curious. Some of them climbed down to see the human baby. MacKinnon stood by as Jamie and the great apes looked at each other. Later, he described that moment as the greatest thrill of his life.

Wouldn't it be fun to be a naturalist? I'll send you a copy of MacKinnon's book. It's called *In Search of the Red Ape*. Read it, so we can learn about orangutans together.

Your friend,
Annick

CHAPTER ONE:

Imagine that you're walking through a rain forest on the island of Borneo. You hear the screech of parrots and the chatter of monkeys. But you're not interested in them today—you're looking for orangutans. Listen for a deep, booming call that echoes through the trees. Follow the sound. If you're lucky, you'll see a male orangutan hanging from his high, leafy perch.

People who see an orangutan for the first time marvel at its "human" appearance. In the native language, orangutan means "man of the woods." That reminds us that humans and orangutans are both primates, and primates are the most advanced of all mammals. Of the thousands of primate species, the great apes (gorillas, chimpanzees, and orangutans) attract the most attention.

Two subspecies of orangutan

Like the gorillas and chimpanzees, orangutans belong to a genus called the *Pongidae*. There are only two subspecies of the orangutan. One lives on the Indone-

Humans and orangutans are both primates, the most advanced of all mammals. This orang is from Borneo.

sian island of Borneo and the other lives on Sumatra. The scientific name for Borneo's orangs is *Pongo pygmaeus pygmaeus*. Their cousins on Sumatra are known as *Pongo pygmaeus abelii*. The Sumatran orang is larger and brighter in color than the Bornean subspecies. It also has longer hair.

An adult male orangutan usually weighs between 150 and 200 pounds (68-91 kg). That's about the same

Orangutans from Sumatra, like this one, are brighter in color than orangs from Borneo.

weight as an average human male. In captivity, some males have grown up to 450 pounds (204 kg)! Adult female orangs are only about one-half the weight of the males. In height, an average male stands about four and one-half feet (1.4 m) tall. The female is usually eight to twelve inches (20-30 cm) shorter.

Female orangs reach their full size when they're about eight years old. Males mature more slowly, passing through a sub-adult stage between the ages of ten and fifteen. When they're fifteen, they start putting on weight and developing their cheek pads and throat pouch. The naturalists who study these great apes say that each one has its own looks and personality.

Reddish hair and cheek pads

An orangutan's bluish-black skin is covered by a thin coat of reddish-brown hair. Its face, ears, palms, and soles are hairless. The coarse hair that covers the rest of its body is thicker on the orang's back and shoulders. This back hair can be up to a foot (30 cm) in length. In addition, orang males often have a beard.

As a male orangutan matures, it develops fleshy pads on its cheeks and forehead. Of all the primates, only the orang has these large pads. As the fatty tissue builds up, the male begins to look as though he's wearing large blinkers. Naturalists think that the pads attract females by making the male look more powerful. It's also possible that the fat stored in the pads serves as a reserve food supply.

Along with their cheek pads, the males develop a bulging throat pouch. The pouch gives their necks a flabby look. This balloon-like sac helps the orang produce the loud bellow known as the "long call." The call warns other males to stay out of their territory. Naturalist Biruté Galdikas says, "The first time I heard the long call I thought I was in the path of a drunken elephant."

Orangs have four hands!

It may sound strange, but an orangutan has four "hands." That's because an orang's toes are just as nimble as its fingers. Both hands and both feet have short thumbs set far down on long, narrow palms. When an orang is swinging from a branch, the four fingers (or toes) curl into a "hook grip." The stumpy little thumbs aren't long enough to help hold on to the branch. The thumbs are also too short to be of much use for picking fruit. But they do come in handy when the orang is breaking off branches to make a nest.

In the trees, the orang uses its hands and feet with

An orangutan uses both its hands and feet when it's in the trees.

almost equal skill. On the ground, however, it's another story. An orang has long arms and short legs. Its armspan can reach seven and one-half feet (2.3 m). That's more than one and a half times its height! When walking, the orang leans forward and walks on all fours. Orangs are able to walk upright, however. They walk on the sides of their feet, with their knees locked. The trained orangs seen in movies adapt to this upright posture fairly easily.

An ape's skull and teeth

An orangutan's skull differs greatly from a human skull. For one thing, its jaw juts far forward and its eye sockets are set close together. The rounded skull holds a brain that is only one-fourth the size of a human brain, but the orang is far from dumb. Adult orangs, for example, carry a "map" of their territory in their heads. The map tells them where each type of fruit grows and when it will ripen.

Orangutan jaws (female left, male right) jut forward more than human jaws.

14

Like human infants, orangutans are toothless when they're born. Their baby teeth develop in their first year. Several years later, large adult teeth replace the baby teeth. The orang's most important teeth are its long, sharp canines (ripping teeth). Four broad, shovel-shaped incisors (cutting teeth) lie between the canines. Their shape makes them useful for scraping fruit pulp from the rind. Ten molars and premolars (grinding teeth) in each jaw complete the orangutan's set of thirty-two teeth.

Senses adapted to the rain forest

The orangutan has a good sense of hearing and excellent color vision. With no serious predators to worry about, it uses its small, rounded ears mostly to listen for the calls of other orangs. As with other fruit-eating primates, the red ape relies on its eyesight to find food. Its large brown eyes quickly search out its favorite fruit, the durian. Since the orang is active only during the day, it hasn't developed good night vision.

Tree-dwelling animals don't usually develop a keen sense of smell. The orangutan, despite its wide, flat nostrils, is no exception. It can detect the normal forest odors, but it doesn't find its food by scent. Smells that would sicken most people don't bother the orang. If spoiled meat, overripe fruit, or rotten eggs are available, the orang will eat them.

Slow and careful

People smile when they first see an orangutan. With its long arms, pot belly, and clownish face, the orang really does look funny. Young orangs like to play, which adds to the fun.

These great apes are very much at home in their native habitat. An orang swings easily from one tree to another on a long, hanging vine. Sometimes it hangs upside down, gripping a branch only with its feet. High above the ground, it tests each new branch before it shifts its weight. A broken branch can mean a fatal fall. Alone in its rain forest habitat, the orangutan isn't in any hurry.

CHAPTER TWO:

Many thousands of years ago, giant orangutans roamed over much of Asia. At that time, dense forests covered much of the continent. Then an ice age sent glaciers moving southward. The water level of the oceans dropped, opening land bridges between the continent and the islands of Indonesia. Driven by the cold, many orangutans moved southward. They found refuge in warmer regions close to the equator.

When the ice age ended, the glaciers melted and the oceans rose. The orangutans were trapped on their tropical islands. Perhaps it was just as well. Those orangs that were left in Asia were probably killed by Stone Age hunters. Even on the islands, the orangs became extinct except on Sumatra and Borneo. These two mountainous islands were not settled for many years. When people did arrive, they tended to stay near the coast.

In Asia, the orang had lived on the ground, like the modern gorilla. But ground-dwelling orangutans couldn't reach the fruit that ripened high in the trees of the rain forest. Only the smaller and lighter orangs survived. Naturalists tell us that today's *Pongo pygmaeus* is only half the size of its long-extinct mainland ancestors.

A hot, damp world

The Indonesian rain forest is a hot, damp world of dense jungle growth. In lands this close to the equator, there are only two seasons—wet and dry. Monsoon rains drop up to 140 inches (356 cm) of rain a year on

Orangutans live in dense rain forests.

Sumatra. In the "dry" months between April and November, the rainfall is reduced by about one-half. At any time of year, the noon temperature can hit ninety degrees Fahrenheit (32 degrees C).

In the rain forest, trees tower more than two hundred feet (61 m) into the air. The orangutan's favorite fruit trees are much smaller, however. Most grow only twenty to seventy feet (6-21 m) tall. They're scattered throughout the forest, a few here and a few there. To make it even harder for the orangs, the fruits don't ripen at the same time. Some trees produce fruit only once in two or three years. This means that the orangs must time their visits carefully—or else go hungry.

A life devoted to fruit

Orangutans are frugivores, which means "fruit-eaters." Some of the fruits they eat are common in the Americas, such as figs and wild plums. Others are tropical fruits, such as lichees, wadans, mangosteens, rambutans, and durians. The bad-smelling durian is one of the orang's favorites. The fruit, which can weigh up to thirty pounds (13.6 kg), has a tough, spiny skin. The orang must strip away the skin to reach the sweet, pulpy flesh.

Orangutans spend much of their time either eating

or looking for food. When they find a tree loaded with ripe fruit, they stay there until they've stripped it of fruit. Only then do they move on to another tree. Since the trees are scattered, only a few orangs can live in any area. Naturalists believe that the limited fruit crop is the reason for the ape's solitary nature. No single area of the forest supplies enough fruit to feed a large troop of orangs.

When fruit is scarce during the wet season, orangutans eat bark, leaves, ferns, and bird eggs. Termites are a special treat during any season. The orang digs into the nest with both hands, scooping up handfuls of the juicy insects. The ape will also seek out a salt lick every month or so. As this varied diet suggests, captive orangutans will eat almost anything. Their huge appetites, combined with a lack of exercise, often cause the males to become very fat.

In the rain forest, finding water to drink is seldom a problem. If there isn't a stream or pool nearby, orangs will scoop water from hollows in the trunks of trees. Crossing a river or swampy area in order to find ripe fruit is a bigger problem. Orangutans don't seem to fear the water, but they can't swim. If the water is shallow, they'll wade across. If it's too deep, they sometimes try to float across on a log. Experiments in zoos have shown that if an orang falls into deep water, it will probably drown.

Orangs spend much of their time looking for fruit in trees.

Clever nest-builders

An orangutan builds a new sleeping nest every night. As the day ends, the animal selects a tall, safe tree. It works quickly, bending branches together to form a solid, springy bed. The branches are never interwoven or knotted. If it's raining, the orang may build a shelter of leafy branches over its head. Naturalists have also seen orangs make simple umbrellas by holding leaves over their heads. Once in its nest, the orang will sleep for up to twelve hours. If two sleeping orangs are sharing a tree, they will almost always be a female and her baby.

The orangutan rises soon after dawn and eats a large breakfast. After one tree has been stripped, the animal moves on to another. For daytime naps, it builds a quick, simple nest. Once its hunger is satisfied, an orangutan may spend some time grooming itself. Females groom their young, but adult orangs seldom groom each other.

"Stay out of my territory"

Most male orangs claim a territory of about two square miles (5 sq. km). Several females usually live within this area. The females have overlapping territories of about 250 acres (100 hectares). If food becomes scarce, orangs leave their homes to find a more fruitful region.

The dominant males lay claim to their territory by using the long call. These calls can last for a minute or more and can be heard for over half a mile (.8 km). When they hear the long call, younger orangs run for cover. The orang sometimes follows the long call with a show of strength called a "display." A male displays

As long as they have food, orangutans will stay in one area.

by ripping off tree branches and throwing them on the ground. When two older males meet, they often display— but they seldom fight. If they do fight, it will likely be over a female who is ready to mate.

An animal with few enemies

In Sumatra, small family groups stay closer together than on Borneo. Naturalists think that's so the big males

An orangutan in the wild can live for forty years or more.

can defend the females and their young from the local leopards and siamang gibbons. These predators don't exist in Borneo.

Orangutans also suffer from fleas, ticks, parasites, and broken bones suffered in falls. Captive orangs face more serious threats. If not cared for properly, they catch pneumonia, malaria, polio, and other human diseases.

Left alone in its habitat, an orangutan may live for forty years or more. Humans haven't always given orangs that freedom. Poachers (illegal hunters) kill the females in order to capture and sell the young apes. In addition, loggers are cutting down the forests for lumber and to clear land for farms.

Fortunately, the Indonesian government has set aside several game preserves for the orangutan. Many of the surviving orangs live in those preserves. If you want to study their life cycle, you may visit them there.

CHAPTER THREE:

Sweat runs down Chris Reynold's face. The young naturalist wipes his forehead and goes back to his notes. Studying orangutans in the rain forest of Borneo is hot work.

Suddenly, a branch crashes down, just missing him. Chris jumps up and moves to a safer spot. "Janie almost got me that time," he mutters to himself. The naturalist watches as the female orangutan breaks off another branch. "I guess the old girl woke up in a bad mood this morning," he thinks.

A misty rain begins to fall. In the steamy rain forests, August is part of the dry season that lasts from March to November. But these "dry" months have their own lighter rains. The really heavy downpours come during the monsoon months of December to February.

An orangutan mates

Janie moves slowly and carefully through the branches. Sometimes she swings arm-over-arm to reach a new bunch of figs. Now the naturalist can see that six-month-old Jack is clinging to the female's chest. When Janie stops to feed, the infant male finds one of her teats and begins to nurse. Jack won't eat solid food until he's a year old.

Chris takes notes on everything the little family does. He gave them all "J" names to separate them from the other family groups he studies. He remembers the time a year ago when Janie mated with Jason. To Chris's surprise, the mating took place in the territory of a large old male. Like many twenty-year-old male orangutans, the fat old ape seemed to have lost interest in mating. Jason was barely ten years old, still a sub-adult. His cheek pads hadn't developed yet. He kept out of the king's way, but he was very active in chasing females.

Jason followed Janie for several days before she allowed him to catch her. Females come into heat every thirty days, but they refuse to mate again until they've raised their young. It was only after four-year-old Joyce went off on her own that Janie showed any interest in mating. Some females wait eight or nine years before giving birth to another infant. Because of this, orangutan populations grow slowly.

The mating took place high in the trees. Chris couldn't help smiling as he watched. Janie was much bigger than Jason. Each time they mated, the usually quiet Janie gave out a loud, sharp cry. Afterward, Jason went his own way. Janie spent her nine months of pregnancy in her usual small territory. Jack was born in a tree nest forty feet (12 m) off the ground. He weighed three and one-half pounds (1.6 kg), about average for an orang. Twins are a rare event in the orangutan's world.

Together but separate

Through his binoculars, Chris now looks at the orangutan's sleeping nest. Last night, it took Janie only ten minutes to gather branches and shape them into a six-

Raising the young is the responsibility of the female orangutan.

foot (1.8 m) nest. Chris knows that Janie won't use the old nest again. Orangutans prefer to build a new nest rather than return to the old one.

An hour later, Janie climbs down to the ground. Following her own mental map of the area, she heads for a grove of durian trees. The coconut-sized fruit has just begun to ripen. Four other orangs are already there. The territory's dominant male, two females, and a two-year-old male are feeding. One of the females is teaching the youngster about eating durians. Orangs have a lot to learn in their first few years of life.

Janie ignores the other orangs. They don't pay attention to her, either. She climbs a tree and begins to feed on the fruit. The odor, like rotten eggs and spoiled meat, doesn't bother her. She ignores the spines and peels off the tough rind. Then she sucks the sweet pulp off the big seeds. Jack gives up the teat to play with one of the seeds.

A battle for status

The peaceful scene changes the instant a second male walks into the clearing. Chris sees that it's Jason. The older male spots him and issues his long call. Jason wants to mate with the younger female. The old male puts on a display. His fur bristles as he rips branches and throws them at Jason. In his fury, he dives forward and swings in a great arc. As he swings, he grips the branch with his feet.

Jason won't back down. He climbs into the tree to challenge the old male. The two orangs wrestle and bite each other on the face and shoulders. When they break apart, Jason chases his opponent through the branches.

Orangutans usually build a new sleeping nest every day.

Female orangutans are loving and protective mothers.

He catches him, but both lose their grip and fall to the ground. Just as quickly, they bounce up and wrestle some more. The fight lasts for thirty minutes. Finally, Jason drags himself away. He's bleeding from a painful wound on his arm. The old male is still king.

The fight upsets Janie, who fears for Jack's safety. Like all female orangs, she is a loving and protective mother. She moves Jack out of sight, then stops to drink from a stream. She licks up a column of tree ants.

32

Finally, it's time for her noontime nap. She builds a simple daytime nest. Jack plays around the edge of the nest for a while. Overhead, the midday sun breaks through the rainclouds.

Chain saws break the silence

A harsh, angry sound wakes Janie an hour later. Chris hears it, too, and frowns. It's the whine of a chain saw. Loggers have invaded the forest to cut down the valuable hardwood trees. Janie moves away from the hated sound. She heads for higher ground, far from the loggers.

As Chris follows, he wonders if the orangs can survive this invasion on their habitat. "At least we didn't meet any poachers today," he says to himself. "The loggers only destroy the forest. Poachers kill the females in order to capture the babies."

By sunset, Janie is far from the chain saws. Moving steadily on the ground, she has traveled six miles (9.7 km). Safe in the quiet forest, she settles into a tall tree. It's time to build her nighttime nest.

A tribe of long-nosed proboscis monkeys swings by. Jack's bright eyes follow their movements curiously. But Janie doesn't pay any attention. She's tired after her flight from danger. She cuddles Jack in her arms and settles down to sleep.

CHAPTER FOUR:

An old Asian story says that the gods created all life on earth. On one of their best days, they made human beings. When the next day came, the gods weren't feeling well. They tried again, but forgot the recipe. Instead of more humans, they created orangutans.

Even today, some natives believe a second myth. They say that orangs are people who displeased the gods. To punish them, the gods gave them red fur and sent them off to live in the rain forest.

Europe learns about orangs

Europeans didn't learn about the great red apes until the early 1600's. Dr. Jakob Bontius reported the first sighting. He said that orangs walked upright, and that they tried to cover up their nakedness!

A better description of the "orang-utan" reached Europe in 1718. An English sea captain named Daniel Beeckman reported, "They are up to six feet (1.8 m) tall, walk upright on their feet, have longer arms than man, and have a tolerable face. They also have large teeth, no tails, and have hair only in those places where man also has hair.''

Beeckman took a young orang to keep him company on his ship. The orang proved to be a clever thief. When no one was looking, it liked to sneak a drink of brandy from Beeckman's cabin.

Until the mid-1800's, Borneo, the apes' home, remained largely unknown to Europeans. In 1839, however, the sultan of Brunei (a province of Borneo) made a deal with a British soldier-of-fortune named James Brooke. The sultan offered to make Brooke the ruler of Sarawak in northwest Borneo—if he could put down a rebellion there. Brooke managed to bring peace to the land. Then he became interested in the orang.

The reports Brooke sent back to London interested other scientists. One of them was Alfred Wallace, who came out to Borneo to see the great apes for himself. Although he was a good scientist, Wallace made several mistakes in his notes on the orang. He said that they rarely leave their trees, and that they cannot walk upright.

Orangutan's enemy: Humans

In remote areas of Borneo, native tribes had always hunted the orangutan for food. When the scientists came, they shot orangs in order to study them. But the greatest slaughter came when hunters arrived in the late 1800's. Captain Rodney Mundy killed several females who were trying to rescue their badly wounded young. An American hunter came to collect orangs and left with nearly fifty animals, dead and alive. The orangutans

In the early 1900's, many female orangs were killed so their young could be captured and sent to zoos.

could not breed fast enough to keep up with their losses. They became extinct in areas where they had once been counted in the hundreds.

The danger to wild orangutans increased in the 1900's. Zoos wanted live orangs for display, and prices for the animals shot upward. Because wild adults couldn't live in captivity, native hunters had to capture the young. But females guard their young with their lives. The hunters had to kill the females in order to take the babies.

Catching young orangs was only the first step. Natives didn't know how to care for them while they waited to make a sale. Many died of hunger or disease. More died on the long boat trip across the Pacific.

The loss of habitat was another serious problem. Farmers began cutting down the rain forest. Rain forest land is not very fertile, however. The sun bakes the thin topsoil, and rain washes it away. Then the farmers must clear another section. Logging crews also destroyed orangutan habitat. Even when they didn't cut down the fruit trees, they upset the ecology of the forest. By 1960, the orangs had been pushed to the edge of extinction.

The world rallies to save the orangutan

For a while, some people thought that orangs could be bred in zoos and then returned to the wild. But this wasn't the case. Although zoos own over two hundred orangs, fewer than ten babies are born each year. Just to keep the zoo population at its current level requires the capture of more wild orangs each year. Experts think that for every infant that reaches a zoo, two orangs die.

Only about 2,500 orangutans now survive on Borneo and Sumatra. The orang is extinct in many areas. Many of the survivors live in game preserves set up by the Indonesian government. The nation isn't rich, however, and saving an endangered species is costly.

Luckily, people all around the world have given time and money to save the orangutan. A number of naturalists have spent their lives studying this least-known of all the great apes. Biruté Galdikas has gone even further. She runs a "rehab center" for captive and orphan orangs.

People from all over the world have helped save the orangutan.

CHAPTER FIVE:

Biruté Galdikas and Rod Brindamour were a little worried about their son, Binti or "Bin." In most ways, Bin was a healthy, normal three-year-old. But the boy walked and made faces just like a young orangutan. Sometimes he even bit people.

Biruté and Rod weren't as worried as most parents would have been. They lived on a game preserve at Tanjung Puting in southern Borneo. Their "rehab center" cared for injured and orphaned orangs until the apes were ready to return to the wild. It was natural for Bin to copy the orangs' behavior.

Who's human and who's an ape?

The two naturalists love their orangutans very much. After a while, Biruté says, she forgets that they're not human. After all, they use tools, want attention, like hugs, and love junk food. They're curious about everything. Give an orang a tin bowl, and it will wear the bowl like a hat.

Princess, an orphan orang who was almost Bin's age, grew up with the boy. Like Bin, Princess held tightly to "mom." The little ape thought that Biruté was her mother. Aside from wanting to be loved, however, Bin and Princess developed in different ways. Bin was interested in everything around him. He picked things up and handled them. When he saw Rod using a tool, he tried to use it, too. But Princess spent most of her time looking for things to eat. Unless Bin was hungry, he gave his food to her.

Learning to "talk"

By his first birthday, Bin was walking and using a few words. Even when he wasn't talking, he made babbling baby sounds. But Princess made very few noises. She squealed when she was hungry or angry. She grunted or chuckled when she was happy, but that was all. Bin may have copied some orang behaviors, but he was clearly human. He walked upright, used tools, learned to speak, and shared his food.

Bin was clearly ahead of Princess in brain power, but the little orangutan had her own strengths. She was stronger than Bin, and she could outclimb him. Fast and shifty, she could make a bigger mess than any human child. Biruté thought that Princess could even learn to "talk!"

In 1916, William Furness had taught a young orang to say "papa" and "cup." The orang used the words properly, but its mouth and tongue couldn't shape more complex words. Later, Gary Shapiro came to Tanjung Puting to teach Ameslan (American Sign Language) to the orangutans. Gary knew that the great apes can learn hundreds of signs for every word they learn to speak.

Princess joined two other orangs in Gary's classes. She quickly learned the signs that asked people to give her more food! No one taught Ameslan to Bin, but he learned the same signs. Instead of talking out loud to Princess, he signed to her.

This orangutan has learned to chew gum!

Growing up human

Biruté and Rod had to keep a close eye on Bin. Left alone, he would try to follow Princess up into the trees. Bin was too young to understand that tree climbing was dangerous. Even the orangs sometimes fell. One female, just released from her cage, quickly climbed a sixty-foot (18 m) tree. A rotten vine broke under her weight and she crashed to the ground. Rod had to put a cast on her broken arm.

As Bin grew older, he made friends with other children. He began to give up his orangutan behaviors. His speech improved and he learned all the skills that humans need. Princess grew up, too. She learned to build a nest and find food in the wild. In time, she would learn to care for her babies. But she would never learn any more than that.

A long-term study

As Bin grew up, the center changed, too. When Biruté started the project, she had only one bark-covered jungle hut. As her work became known, university students joined her. They put up new buildings and made lists of more than three hundred foods eaten by orangutans. They cared for the center's "rehabs" and carefully studied orangutan behavior.

The Indonesian Forestry Department sent scientists and workers to join the project. This support was part of a government effort to save its endangered apes. After years of neglect, officials finally began to enforce strict laws against poachers. When they found captive orangs, they took them to the rehab center.

Biruté knows that her work is just beginning. A few orangs live as long as fifty years, and her study is only fifteen years old. By the time she finishes, she hopes that the great red apes will be off the endangered species list.

Biruté works very hard to take care of her orangutans. She knows that the world would be a poorer place without these shy, funny-looking ''red apes.''

This photo shows experts at work in Indonesia at an orangutan research project.

The world just wouldn't be the same without these funny-looking "red apes."

MAP:

The shaded areas
on this map show
where orangutans
are found on the
islands of Sumatra
and Borneo.

INDEX/GLOSSARY:

INDEX/GLOSSARY:

WILDLIFE
HABITS & HABITAT

If you would like to know more about all kinds of wildlife, you should take a look at the other books in this series.

You'll find books on bald eagles and other birds. Books on alligators and other reptiles. There are books about deer and other big-game animals. And there are books about sharks and other creatures that live in the ocean.

In all of the books you will learn that life in the wild is not easy. But you will also learn what people can do to help wildlife survive. So read on!